Denver
Travel Guide

Quick Trips Series

No part of this publication may be reproduced, stored in a retrieval system, or transmitted, in any form or by any means without the prior written permission of the publisher, nor be otherwise circulated in any form of binding or cover other than that in which it is published and without similar condition being imposed on the subsequent purchaser. If there are any errors or omissions in copyright acknowledgements the publisher will be pleased to insert the appropriate acknowledgement in any subsequent printing of this publication. Although we have taken all reasonable care in researching this book we make no warranty about the accuracy or completeness of its content and disclaim all liability arising from its use.

Copyright © 2016, Astute Press
All Rights Reserved.

Table of Contents

DENVER — 6
- Customs & Culture 7
- Geography 9
- Weather & Best Time to Visit 11

SIGHTS & ACTIVITIES: WHAT TO SEE & DO — 13
- City Park 13
- Denver Art Museum 16
- LoDo District 17
- Colorado Railroad Museum 18
- Echo Lake & Mount Evans 19
- Georgetown 20
- Confluence Park 23
- Cherokee Ranch & Castle Foundation 24
- Dinosaur Ridge 26
- Museum of Denver 28

BUDGET TIPS — 34
- Accommodation 34

Residence Inn Denver City Center 34
Holiday Inn Express Denver Aurora-Medical Center 35
Warwick Hotel 36
Embassy Suites, Downtown & Convention Center 37
Magnolia Hotel 39

🌐 Restaurants, Cafés & Bars 40

Bang! 40
Zaidy's Deli 41
Steuben's 42
Mead St. Station 43
Osteria Marco 44

🌐 Shopping 46

16th Street Mall 46
Tabor Center 46
Cherry Creek Shopping District 47
Antique Row 48
South Pearl Street 49

KNOW BEFORE YOU GO   51

🌐 Entry Requirements 51

🌐 Health Insurance 52

🌐 Traveling with Pets 53

🌐 Airports 55

🌐 Airlines 59

🌐 Hubs 62

🌐 Seaports 64

🌐 Money Matters 66

🌐 Currency 66

🌐 Banking/ATMs 66

🌐 Credit Cards 67

🌐 Tourist Tax 68

- Sales Tax 69
- Tipping 70
- Connectivity 71
- Mobile Phones 71
- Dialing Code 73
- Emergency Numbers 73
- General Information 73
- Public Holidays 73
- Time Zones 74
- Daylight Savings Time 76
- School Holidays 76
- Trading Hours 77
- Driving 77
- Drinking 79
- Smoking 80
- Electricity 81
- Food & Drink 82
- American Sports 84
- Useful Websites 86

DENVER TRAVEL GUIDE

Denver

Denver, the capital of Colorado, is nicknamed the Mile High City at 5,280 feet (1 mile) above sea level in the Rocky Mountains. The city's neighborhoods include LoDo (Lower Downtown), Capitol Hill, Highland, Washington Park, Baker and Lowry. With its green city parklands, the impressive Rocky Mountains as a backdrop and the

DENVER TRAVEL GUIDE

nonstop urban day and nightlife, Denver is a hub of activity that is sure to thrill the visitor.

The largest city in Colorado is located just to the east of the Front Range of the Rocky Mountains and west of the High Plains. This makes the city mostly flat to the west side and hilly throughout the rest.

Denver has over 80 neighborhoods and more than 200 green parks to enjoy on a sunny, clear day. These parks are often the focal points of the neighborhoods. City Park is the largest park in Denver and is 314 acres in size. Denver has more than 4,000 acres of parks plus an additional 14,000 acres of mountain parks.

🌏 Customs & Culture

With a large Hispanic population, Denver hosts some major Mexican-American celebrations. In May there is a large Cinco de Mayo festival that attracts over 500,000 people. In September visit the El Grito de la Independcia, the celebration of Mexican Independence. Denver also hosts the Lowrider festival and the Dia De Los Muertos art show. At these events or on a regular trip try Denver's famous Southwestern cuisine.

With Denver being so close to the mountains many visitors spend their time taking advantage of the beautiful natural environment. The winter weekends are often filled with people skiing in the mountains to the west of Denver. In the warmer months vistors will enjoy hiking or climbing in the mountains. Many take advantage of the location to go kayaking or camping.

DENVER TRAVEL GUIDE

Asian-American festivals are popular in Denver. The Chinese New Year has a large celebration. The Dragon Boat festival is in July. September is when locals host the Moon Festival. Denver also has two Chinese newspapers.

Denver is the setting for some well-known television shows. The show Dynasty was set in Denver. The Bill Engvall Show which stared comedian Bill Engvall was set in Denver though it was filmed in Los Angeles. The Disney Channel currently has a show which is set in Denver called Good Luck Charlie. It is also where the show E-Vet Interns takes place. The ABC original show starring Tim Allen is set in Denver as is the ABC Family series Make it or Break it.

DENVER TRAVEL GUIDE

🌎 Geography

Denver is nestled between the great Rocky Mountains to its west and the High Plains to its east. With only being a few miles from the Front Range of the Rocky Mountains Denver is a very hilly city. It is also the most populated city in Colorado and indeed is the most populous city within a 500 mile radius.

With Denver being so large it is made up of eighty neighborhoods. Some of the more well-known neighborhoods are the historical and trendy LoDo. This neighborhood is made up of a little more than a 23 square block radius that was the original location of Denver.

Another well-known neighborhood is Highland which is in north Denver. This is one of the most sought after areas to live in Denver with its proximity to LoDo making it

DENVER TRAVEL GUIDE

appealing. Capitol Hill is where the artists and bohemians hang out. It is a place filled with galleries, bars, clubs, and restaurants. With two concert venues the neighborhood is also known for having a wild nightlife. With the gay pride parade going through the neighborhood every year the neighborhood has also been called the gay village.

Denver has many bicycle commuters and many streets have bicycle lanes. When you add this to the over 850 miles of paved bike paths you can see why Denver is so bicycle friendly. The city even started a Bicycle program where for a small fee people can check out a bicycle, much like a library allows you to check out a book. You can rent for 24 hours, 7 days, 30 days, or one year. The cost of membership depends on how long you want to ride the bicycle. This will make it easier for those people who are on vacation who want to use a bike.

DENVER TRAVEL GUIDE

The public transportation is operated by Regional Transportation District (RTD). The RTD have over 1,000 buses. These buses cover 38 districts that are in 8 different counties. They are also putting into effect FasTracks which will soon give commuters the opportunity to travel by train. FasTracks hopes to be up and running before 2016.

🌎 Weather & Best Time to Visit

Denver has four distinct seasons and with Denver being located so close to the Rocky Mountains it can have sudden changes in weather. The warmest month of the year for Denver is July with the average temperature being 90 degrees Fahrenheit (32 degrees Celsius) and the average low being 60 degrees Fahrenheit (16 degrees Celsius). December is the coldest month with highs only

DENVER TRAVEL GUIDE

reaching 44 degrees Fahrenheit (7 degrees Celsius) and the low falling 18 degrees Fahrenheit (-8 degrees Celsius). The average first snowfall is October 18 and the last snowfall averages around April 30. Denver actually has 300 days of sunshine.

With all the different festivals that Denver hosts you can go at any time of the year and enjoy it. Though many like to take advantage of the closeness of the mountains. If hiking, camping, climbing or kayaking are what you are looking for then travel to Denver in late spring or during the summer. If you are wanting to ski then the winter months are for you.

DENVER TRAVEL GUIDE

Sights & Activities: What to See & Do

🌎 City Park

City Park is the largest park in Denver and is 330 acres in size located in east-central Denver. City Park has at two lakes; Ferril Lake and Duck Lake and also a boathouse. The two biggest attractions that City Park features are the Denver Zoo and the Denver Museum of Nature and Science which makes it a great way to spend the day rain or shine.

DENVER TRAVEL GUIDE

Denver Zoo is on over 80 acres of land inside City Park. There is a bicycle kiosk at the zoo entrance so you can choose to bike your way through if you want. This zoo is open 365 days out of the year and there are almost 4,000 animals to be seen. These animals are from 700 different species which means that you can see animals here that you would not see in other zoos. Admission price runs anywhere from free to $15. The zoo also offers free days, you can check the website to see if there is a free day when you plan to visit Denver. In the summer months admission to the zoo is open from 9am to 5pm with the grounds staying open until 6pm. Should you choose to go in the winter months admission is open from 10 am to 4pm with the grounds staying open until 5pm.

DENVER TRAVEL GUIDE

Shows and exhibits are scheduled throughout the day. At 10am and 2:30 pm you can catch the Sea Lion Show. Then at 10:45am and again at 2pm is the Toyota Elephant Passage Demonstration. Also at 2pm is Africa's Greatest Predators. Tropical Discovery and Bird World is open from 10am to 5pm. Outside of Bird World at 10:15am and 3:30 pm is African Penguin Feeding. If you want to see the Lorikeet Adventure then plan your visit for the weekend. It is from 10am to 3:30 pm Friday, Saturday and Sunday. If you have children they will enjoy the carousel ride and the train.

For more information about the Denver Zoo you feel free to stop by their website. http://www.denverzoo.org/

The other major attraction at City Park is the Denver Museum of Nature and Science which was established in

DENVER TRAVEL GUIDE

1900. This museum is open every day of the year except December 25 from 9am to 5pm. Admission prices vary depending on what part of the museum you want to see. You can check admission prices here http://www.dmns.org/plan-your-visit/ticket-prices/.

There are several current exhibitions at the museum and some rotating ones. By checking the museum's website you can see which exhibits will be available when you visit. Expedition Health is a place where you not only learn about the human body but you learn about your own body. This exhibit allows you to examine some of your own cells, it is an interactive exhibit. Space Odyssey is a unique exhibit since it lets you see things as they would be seen from outer space. Egyptian Mummies, Gems and Minerals, North American Indian Culture, and Wildlife

DENVER TRAVEL GUIDE

exhibits are all ones that are among the permanent collection.

You can catch shows at the Planetarium and the IMAX. If you get hungry stop by the T-Rex Café or Grab & Go. For more information on the Denver Museum of nature and Science feel free to stop by the website http://www.dmns.org/ or call 303.370.6000. It is located in City Park at 2001 Colorado Blvd.

Denver Art Museum

The Denver Art Museum is located at 100 W. 14th Ave. Parkway in Denver. This museum is open from 10am to 5pm Tuesday through Thursday, Saturday and Sunday. On Friday the hours are from 10am to 8pm. Mondays it is closed. On the first Saturday of every month admission is

DENVER TRAVEL GUIDE

free. Admission price ranges from free (0-5 years old) to $13.

There are always new exhibits rotating at the museum and there are 13 permanent collections. These include African Art, American Indian Art, Architecture Design & Graphics, Asian Art, European and American Art, the Logan Collection, Modern and Contemporary Art, Oceanic Art, Photography, Pre-Columbian Art, Spanish Colonial Art, Textile Art, and Western American Art. These exhibits are sure to please any art lover.

For the visitors with children there are daily activities. Just for Fun Center is a place where children can try on costumes and play with color. There are more children friendly activities but they are not always offered. It is best to check the website at http://www.denverartmuseum.org/.

DENVER TRAVEL GUIDE

🌐 LoDo District

The LoDo (Lower Downtown) district is the historical part of Denver and is located where Denver was originally built. It is now a trendy place to visit and live. It has 90 brewpubs, sports bars, rooftop cafes and restaurants. LoDo also has some terrific shops. If you are interested in the history of Denver then maybe a walking tour is for you. On this guided tour you can learn about the history of the buildings and which buildings were used to house the local saloons, brothels, and the people who owned them. To schedule a walking tour of LoDo visit its website http://www.lodo.org/.

🌐 Colorado Railroad Museum

The Colorado Railroad Museum is worth the 25 minute drive to Golden, Colorado. It is located at 17155 West 44th Avenue in Golden, Colorado. This unique museum is one

DENVER TRAVEL GUIDE

that every train lover will enjoy. The locomotives are not just for looking at, they are operational. Not only can you look at these trains but you can also go for a ride. On most Saturdays you can go for a ride on the 1/3 mile track which will give you a different view of the roundhouse and turntable. Like model trains then stop by the train garden or check out the Denver HO Society model railroad which is located on the lower level of the main building. Here the layout is much like the railroads of historical Colorado.

These trains are operated by a member of the Denver HO Society on Tuesdays. If you have a little one who adores Thomas the Train then check the website to see if Day Out With Thomas is going on when you will be in the Denver area. Check out the website to see if there are any special events going on when you plan your visit http://coloradorailroadmuseum.org/. Admission ranges

DENVER TRAVEL GUIDE

from free to $10. If you have a family then check out the family admission rate of $30 which covers two adults and up to five children under the age of 16. The museum is open from 9am to 5pm year round with special holiday hours on Easter, Christmas Eve, and New Year's Eve. They are closed Christmas day, New Year's Day and Thanksgiving.

🌎 Echo Lake & Mount Evans

Mount Evans is called "the road to the stars" as it is the highest paved automobile road in America. Drive the 14 miles to the Mount Evans summit parking lot. Once there you can hike ¼ mile to the top of Mount Evans. Mount Evans is 14,264 feet high and telling your friends that you climbed that mountain would impress. The road to the top of Mount Evans starts at Echo Lake. This beautiful mountain lake is known as a great fishing spot. A trail

DENVER TRAVEL GUIDE

going around the lake is ¾ of a mile long. There are some beautiful picnic grounds near the lake. The road is closed from October to May due to snow.

You can still hike, bike, or even snow-shoe along trails. If you want to stay overnight there are several campgrounds at different elevations. Access fees for motorized vehicles depend on the number of passengers. The access pass is good for 3 days. The fees can go as high as $40. For more information and to see if the road is open at the time of your visit please stop by the website http://www.mountevans.com/index.html.

🌐 Georgetown

Georgetown is 42 miles west of Denver but worth the drive. Georgetown started out as a mining camp in 1859. Once popular because of its potential to make you rich it

DENVER TRAVEL GUIDE

is now popular because of its location. It has beautiful views of the Rocky Mountains. No matter what your interests you will be able to find something to do in Georgetown. In the winter months there is ice fishing, ice racing; for those of you who enjoy ice skating you can do that at Werlin Park. There is always skiing and snowboarding.

The warmer months are filled with activities. Spend the day relaxing while fishing at Georgetown Lake. The lake is stocked with trout, rainbows, Brookes, and browns. There are limits on the size and number of fish so be sure to check out Georgetown's website if fishing will be on your agenda. Travel the old mining trails on ATVs with the Mountains ATV Tours. Visit in June and you can participate in the Slacker Half Marathon Races. These races are all downhill and proceeds go to local charities.

DENVER TRAVEL GUIDE

Whitewater rafting can be done at two locations Arkansas River and Clear Creek.

A day and evening of leisure can be found in Georgetown, perfect for a romantic date or to enjoy with friends and family. Start your day off with a Victorian Garden Tour where several historic homes are opened to you so you can see what life was like during the early years of the mining town. Then from 10am to 6pm you can stop by Canyon Wind Cellars for winetasting. Taste several different wines or enjoy a glass of your favorite along with a cheese plate. Next, top your evening off with a night at the opera at The Central City Opera House. This is a beautifully restored theatre that will be well worth the drive. It is around 30 minutes from Georgetown, at least it is on its way back to Denver with only a slight detour.

DENVER TRAVEL GUIDE

Georgetown has 3 museums. Stop by the Hotel De Paris Museum will send you back in time to 1875. The Hammil House Museum is a magnificent example of a Country Style Gothic Revival house. The Georgetown Electric Museum is an operating hydroelectric plant that was built in 1900.

Don't forget to take advantage of the Georgetown Loop Railroad. These open passenger cars pulled by a steam locomotive give you a wonderful view of the mountains and gold/silver mines while you are on your way up the canyon to Silver Plume.

To find out about more of any of these activities check out Georgetown's website. You may want to plan on spending an entire day here. http://www.georgetown-colorado.org/main.htm

DENVER TRAVEL GUIDE

🌎 Confluence Park

Confluence Park is where Denver was originally founded as a mining camp in 1858. Now it is the center of Denver's 850 mile bike trail way. This park in downtown Denver is located next to the South Platte River and Cherry Creek. There is a large outdoor amphitheater for park concerts. With a nice beach and plenty of green space this park is perfect for picnics. You can go kayaking on the Platte River. If you want to see fire performers and drummers practice fire spinning by the water then you want to head to the Confluence Park on a warm Tuesday or Friday night.

🌎 Cherokee Ranch & Castle Foundation

The Cherokee Ranch and Castle Foundation is located outside of Denver in Sedalia. The 1450s Scottish style

DENVER TRAVEL GUIDE

castle was built by the Johnson family in 1924. They later sold their homestead to Tweet Kimball in 1954, he also purchased the neighboring homestead and combined the two.

The castle holds several performances a year. Some types of performances are murder-mystery, theatrical, jazz, classical, family, and special performances. The website has a calendar that can be checked for performances. If you want a guided tour they are $15 per person and offered for kids (fourth grade and older) and adults on Wednesdays, Thursdays, and Saturdays. These are typically an hour and a half long. While on the tour you will hear about the history of the castle, the people who built it and inhabited it, you will see its collection of art form around the world and the unique furnishing that fill the castle.

DENVER TRAVEL GUIDE

Ever wanted tea in a castle? Now is your chance. Tea is again offered to those in fourth grade or older. The cost is $42 per person. There is a seasonal menu. Of course you will get scones with clotted cream and jam, finger sandwiches, and pastries. Tea is served every other Wednesday or Saturday from 2pm to 4pm. You can also request a private tea for birthdays, bridal showers, or just outings with your friends or family.

The castle also offers hikes, whisky tasting, summer camps for adults and children alike. To find out more about these check out their website for the newest schedule.

303-688-5555

6113 Daniels Park Rd.

DENVER TRAVEL GUIDE

Sedalia, 80135

http://www.cherokeeranch.org/

🌐 Dinosaur Ridge

Want a fun and educational experience? Visit Dinosaur Ridge and see the creatures who use to roam Colorado. Hike the Dinosaur Ridge trail way, this hike will take anywhere from 1 to 2 hours. Along the way stop at up to 15 different spots of interest. These spots include fossils, scenic overlooks, and interesting rock formations. At the Dinosaur Ridge Track site you can see actual fossilized dinosaur tracks. You can also learn more about it at the Trek Through Time exhibit. Want to touch a dinosaur bone then head over to the Bone Quarry where you will find dinosaur bones fossilized in rock.

DENVER TRAVEL GUIDE

Walking the gravel Triceratops Trail you will see 3-D triceratops footprints. This trail is a little harder to walk and not likely passable for those who are disabled. Not only will you see footprints on this trail but you will see fossils of plants imbedded into the rock.

Backyard Bones: Dinosaur Dig Pit is perfect for younger ones. It allows children to dig much like a paleontologist would. They will discover bones and then investigate to find out why the dinosaur they found was there.

Trek Through Time Dinosaur Exhibit Hall is a place where you can go to discover even more about dinosaurs. The Cost is only $2 per person, three and younger get in for free. Here you will find five murals, fossils that have been dug up and placed behind glass to keep them safe, and interactive exhibits. If you get hungry during your visit stop

DENVER TRAVEL GUIDE

by The Stegosaurus Snack Shack which is located next to the gift shop. For more information and to check for special events, dates and times that these areas are open check out the website.

303-697-3466

16831 W. Alameda Pkwy

Morrison, 80465

http://www.dinoridge.org/index.html

Museum of Denver

The Children's Museum of Denver is open from 9am to 4pm, Monday through Friday; staying open until 7pm on Wednesdays. Saturday and Sunday you can come play from 10am to 5pm. Admission ranges from $7 to $9. This is a place where children can play and learn at the same time. There are 15 playscapes all of which are designed

DENVER TRAVEL GUIDE

to be fun for everyone though they have target age groups.

3,2,1...Blast Off! This is a wonderful place for a young, aspiring astronaut. Here children can build their own rockets and launch them. They can also view a video of real rocket launches. The wind tunnel is a place where the children can place different colored scarves to see how the wind moves them. This is fun for all though it was designed with those between the ages of 2 and 8 in mind.

Bubbles is a playscape where children will learn about shapes, mixtures, force, and evaporation. They will use not only their large and fine motor skills but will use mathematics and science. At the Big Bubble Maker you can make bubbles that are over 6 feet long! The Drop Zone is where you can pop vapor-filled bubbles. You can

DENVER TRAVEL GUIDE

fill bubbles with vapor mist at the Vapor Station. There are so many more wonderful things to do and explore in this playscape. This is for all ages but the educational aspect of it is geared towards those 6 to 8 years of age.

Just Add Water is a fun water exhibit where you will get wet. It is a good idea to have a towel handy or even clothes that will dry quickly. This water exhibit is not a place or swimming, it is a place for learning and having fun. Here children will learn about geysers, whirlpools and fountains. Here children can work pumps, they can channel, and they can sprinkle water. They can even paint with it. The target age group is 1 t 8 but this would be fun for all especially on a hot day.

Spotlights is where you can explore color and movement. When you step onto the floor you immediately get a colored spotlight that follows you around when you move. Your color stays the same, other people on the floor will have other colors. When you get close to someone your circles will combine and the colors will blend. Learn how two colors can make a new color in this fun interactive exhibit.

The Art Studio is designed for those who are between the ages of 2 and 4 though it will be fun for anyone. Here is a place where children can explore their creative side. Let them grab an easel and paint. There are many different types of crafts that can be done here.

The Assembly Plant is targeted for those 4 to 8 years of age. This playscape provides you and your child with all the tools and recyclable materials that you will need to create a new masterpiece. Get settled in a station where

DENVER TRAVEL GUIDE

you can have your own blueprint. Here using the tools will help children with their fine motor skills. If they choose to follow a blueprint then they will have to read and follow the directions.

The Big Backyard is designed for those who are 3 to 6 but again this is something that will be fun for everyone. This oversized backyard will let children see the outside world from the point of view of the creatures who live outside. Let them explore the world of an ant or that of a bird with the costumes that the kids can wear.

Click Clack Train Track will be fun experience for all but it is targeted to 2 to 5 year olds. Here they can put on a conductors hat and build train tracks. Watch your little engineer build a landscape around the train tracks by

DENVER TRAVEL GUIDE

setting up trees. This will be fun for any child who enjoys trains.

Fire Station No. 1 is a wonderful firefighter experience designed to engage those 3 to 6 years of age. Allow your little one to dress up as a fire fighter, get in a fire truck and learn about what it takes to be one of these heroes. This exhibit is pretty much a recreation of a firehouse. The children can see a firefighter's bunk and kitchen, see how they live when they have to stay at the firehouse. Along with the 911 dispatch station there is the always fun fireman's pole. Your children are sure to enjoy this exhibit, when they are tired out from all the playing sit down and look through the fireman's yearbook to see a history of this brave profession.

DENVER TRAVEL GUIDE

While you are at the Children's Museum of Denver do not forget to stop by these other playstations Kinetics where you can experience a life size marble run and Hopscotch where you can draw on a statue of a cow or lay hopscotch with the family.

303-433-7444

2121 Children's Museum Dr.

Denver, 80211

http://www.mychildsmuseum.org/Default.aspx

DENVER TRAVEL GUIDE

DENVER TRAVEL GUIDE

Budget Tips

🌐 Accommodation

Residence Inn Denver City Center

1724 Champa Street

Denver, CO

(303) 296-3444

http://www.marriott.com/hotels/travel/denrd-residence-inn-denver-city-center/

This hotel has a great location as it is within walking distance of many shops, restaurants, entertainment, arts, and sporting events. This hotel rooms feature full suites. Check in is at 4pm and check out is at 11am. There is parking for an extra $25 a day. Take advantage of the complimentary hot buffet style breakfast, room delivery of

DENVER TRAVEL GUIDE

meals from local restaurants and the Bar-B-Q/ picnic area. Each room offers wired and wireless internet. In the evenings there is complimentary beer and wine.

All of the rooms offer air conditioning, iron and ironing board, cable television, coffee/tea service, bottle water (for a fee), the bathroom has a hair dryer. The biggest thing that each room has is a kitchen that is fully equipped with what you would need to cook. The hotel offers grocery delivery for a fee.

Prices start at $199 a night which gives you a queen bed and a sofa bed. The rates go as high as $319 a night which gives you a 2 room suite; two bedrooms with queen size beds, a sofa bed, and two bathrooms.

DENVER TRAVEL GUIDE

Holiday Inn Express Denver Aurora-Medical Center

1500 South Abilene Street

Aurora, Colorado

(303) 369-8400

http://www.ihg.com/holidayinnexpress/hotels/us/en/aurora/denac/hoteldetail

Only 20 minutes from the Denver International Airport and less than 30 minutes away from LoDo this hotel is in a great location. You can catch a sporting event or go shopping in LoDo. They offer a complimentary hot breakfast. Though there is no restaurant in the hotel there are several restaurants nearby. There is an on-site fitness center and an outdoor pool. Each room offers cable television, pay-per-view movies, in room video games are available, and kitchenette. There is a work desk and high-speed internet access. The room rates start at low as $79 a night.

Warwick Hotel

1776 Grant Street

Denver, Colorado

(303) 861-2000

http://www.warwickdenver.com/

This hotel luxurious hotel is located on the edges of the Uptown and Capitol Hill neighborhoods. This puts it away from the noise but still close enough that you do not have to travel far to get to great restaurants, shopping, and clubs. The hotel offers many amenities including Randolph's Restaurant and Bar. Take advantage of the heated rooftop pool. You can even check out the gift shop. The hotel offers high-speed internet access. There

DENVER TRAVEL GUIDE

is a fitness center, same day laundry service, and 24 hour room service.

The rooms offer wireless or wired internet access, 32 inch televisions, cable with HBO, honor bar, floor to ceiling glass doors to the balcony, and balcony furniture. There are robes and slippers in the rooms. All of this for a price starting at $129 a night.

Embassy Suites, Downtown & Convention Center

1420 Stout Street

Denver, Colorado

(303) 592-1000

http://embassysuites3.hilton.com/en/hotels/colorado/embassy-suites-denver-downtown-convention-center-DENESES/index.html

DENVER TRAVEL GUIDE

This hotel is within walking distance of downtown. You are close to the attractions of downtown Denver when staying here. It is close to the 16th Street Mall and the Theatrical District. Some of the great things this hotel offers are the indoor pool and fitness center. Looking for a place to relax but not wanting to go to your room yet? Check out the hotel bar and lounge.

Each room has a private bedroom and a living room. Enjoy the microwave, wet bar, fridge, and the two televisions that are in every suite. Each suite has internet access, a desk, air conditioning, a complimentary paper on weekdays, and pay per view movies. Cribs and toddler beds are available upon request.

DENVER TRAVEL GUIDE

Rates start as low as $99 a night. If you want a room with a mountain view be prepared to pay a little more.

Magnolia Hotel

818 17th Street

Denver, Colorado

(303) 607-9000

http://www.magnoliahotels.com/denver/magnolia-hotel-denver.php

This hotel is in a historic bank building. It is only a block away from the 16th Street Mall. Summit County's four ski areas are an hour drive away. This makes it a great location for those who have come to Denver to enjoy the slopes. There are some wonderful room amenities. High speed internet access, flat screen television, pay-per-view movies and Nintendo, in room coffee and tea, and

DENVER TRAVEL GUIDE

bathrobes. Eat in the Lounge, at Harry's Bar or order in room service. Rates start as low as $129 a night.

🌐 Restaurants, Cafés & Bars

Bang!

3472 West 32nd Street

Denver, Colorado

(303) 455-1117

http://bangdenver.com/

This restaurant serves high quality dishes without the high price tag. Instead of an open kitchen the kitchen has a street view. The cooks are on display for everyone to see.

The menu here changes two to three times a year. Here you will find comfort food with Southern flair. Favorites that are on the menu all year round are gumbo and spicy, peppered shrimp, and grilled salmon.

Here is where you can find sweet potato bread and hush puppies which you will not find just anywhere in Denver. They have a $5 kids menu. When going to eat at Bang! keep an eye out for the entrance which is located in a narrow alleyway. On nice days the patio is filled with people. This restaurant is located perfectly, it is on a man street but positioned in such a way that there is not much street noise.

Zaidy's Deli

1512 Larimer Street

Denver, Colorado

(303) 893-3600

http://www.zaidysdeli.com/default.aspx

DENVER TRAVEL GUIDE

This is a kosher deli that has two locations in Denver the main restaurant is located off of Writer's Square off the 16th Street Mall, the second location is on Adam's Street.

This casual deli is open from 6:30 am to 3:00 pm daily. They offer breakfast and lunch. Check out the box lunches which all come with your choice of potato salad, coleslaw or chips a pickle, fresh fruit, and a homemade cookie. Bread choices are pumpernickel, whole wheat, rye, sour dough, and Kaiser Roll. The most expensive box lunch is $12.95.

Be sure to check out the dessert menu with its pies, cookies, cheesecakes, rice pudding and cookies. While looking for something to drink, try the egg cream.

DENVER TRAVEL GUIDE

Steuben's

523 East 17th Street

Denver, Colorado

(303) 830-1001

http://www.steubens.com/

Steuben's is a classic American comfort food. This is a popular restaurant so if expect about a 30 minute wait. If there are 6 or more in your group then call ahead for a reservation. Sundays are the busiest day for this place.

Classic comfort food is what this restaurant strives for. With items on the menu like macaroni and cheese, fried chicken, baked ziti, and flat iron steak among several other choices everyone is bound to find something that will delight their taste buds and remind them of home.

DENVER TRAVEL GUIDE

Here is another restaurant where you can pick up an egg cream. Steuben's also offers allergy menus for those with food allergies. Be sure to tell your waiter or waitress if you have a food allergy.

Mead St. Station

3625 W. 3nd Avenue

Denver, Colorado

(303) 433-2138

http://www.meadststation.com/

Mead St. Station is a bar that is equipped with a full kitchen. During the day you will find people inside enjoying a meal. At night the place really comes to life with music. Here not only can you get a meal but a drink too.

DENVER TRAVEL GUIDE

With an extensive menu you are bound to find food to satisfy what you are craving and all while enjoying music from local bands. The menu has 11 sections. B.Y.O.B. or build your own burger where you can choose the meat, choose the cheese, and even the toppings. The menu also breaks down to sweets, between the bread, greens & things, drinks & beverages, pub grub, sides, soup, specialty burgers, happy hour menu, and signature plates. Here you will find food like Fish n' Chips, Mead St. Nachos, Fried Pickles, Buffalo Chicken Sandwich, and the soup of the day.

As for entertainment there is something different every night. Monday night is Open Mic Night, if you are up for the challenge and want to be put on the list then give Mead St. Station a call. Tuesday night is Rock n' Roll Bingo where music clips and video clips are played with you trying to match them to your card; there are cash prizes. Wednesday through Saturday night has live music.

Osteria Marco

1453 Larimer

Denver, Colorado

(303) 534-5855

http://www.osteriamarco.com/

This Italian restaurant is one of Denver's best fine casual dining restaurants. It will be good for a date, but also good for a quiet family meal. Here you will find a great chef who creates meals. The chef here was cited as one of "10 Denver chefs you need to know". The restaurant offers indoor and outdoor dining. Try the bruschetta or order a pizza. If Italian food is what you crave this is a good place to go. It has an extensive wine list, I am sure the staff would be happy to help if you are not well versed in wine.

Hours are Monday through Thursday 11am to 10pm, Friday and Saturday 11am to 11pm, and Sunday 11am to 10pm. Call ahead for reservations if you want to be sure to have a table. Plates tend to run in the $15 to $25 range.

🌐 Shopping

16th Street Mall

Downtown Denver

http://16thstreetmalldenver.com/

The 16th Street Mall is in the heart of downtown Denver. It spans 16 blocks. Here is where you will find many stores and some of Denver's best restaurant. Cars are not

DENVER TRAVEL GUIDE

allowed to drive here so people enjoy the large sidewalks. They can also take one of the free shuttles. Here you can find shops such as Virgin Records Megastore, GAP, and Niketown. Restaurants include Hard Rock Café and Maggianno's Little Italy among many others. This is a wonderful outdoors shopping experience.

Tabor Center

1200 17th Street, Suite 610, Denver, Colorado

(303) 628-1000

http://www.taborcenter.com/

This is a hotel and a shopping experience rolled into one. Come to The Tabor Center if you want to not only shop but eat and relax at a spa.

DENVER TRAVEL GUIDE

This modern mall is a wonderful pace to spend a day with some shop therapy. It may not have several stores like other malls but it does have nice boutiques. This is where you will find Secret Garden Florist, Events Dress Boutique and The Shirt Broker. You can also find the Cheesecake Factory in this 3 level mall, office building, and hotel.

Cherry Creek Shopping District

3.5 miles from downtown Denver

http://www.shopcherrycreek.com/

Located in the vicinity of 1st, 2nd, and 3rd Avenues and from University to Steele Street. Here you will find 320 independently owned shops and restaurants. In addition to these are 160 brand name stores. This is the largest, shopping center between San Francisco and Chicago. Here you will find stores in every department. Women's

DENVER TRAVEL GUIDE

Fashions, Toy stores, maternity, luggage, book stores, and so many other types of shops call Cherry Creek home. The Cherry Creek Bike path leads right to the mall. Check the website for a list of stores though I do not think any shopper would be disappointed here.

Antique Row

400-2000 South Broadway

Denver, Colorado

http://www.antique-row.com/

This is an antique lovers paradise. Here you will find 7 blocks of antique dealers, specialty shops, restaurants and more. You will find stores that can keep you busy all day. There are 7 art shops, 11 jewelry shops (which includes Somewhere in Time), 4 bookstores, and 8 toy, doll and collectible shops. There are several more stores.

DENVER TRAVEL GUIDE

After all of your shopping or even between stores stop in at one of the 4 restaurants.

South Pearl Street

1569 South Pearl Street

Denver, Colorado

(303) 282-7777

http://www.southpearlstreet.com/index.html

South Pearl Street is a historic shopping district in Denver. It is also one of the more popular ones. Here you will find stores such as Gracie's where they provide unique and affordable clothing and gifts. The Empty Bottle is a wine shop that specializes in harder to find wines.

Polkadot is a gift shop where you will find items by a local artist. Hungry while you shop then stop by one of the

DENVER TRAVEL GUIDE

several restaurants. Budapest Bistro is where you will find Hungarian food. Stop by Lincoln's Roadhouse if you are in the mood for Cajun or Creole cuisine while enjoying some live Blues or Americana music on the weekends. Sexy Pizza is the place in Denver to find New York style pizza. There are several other restaurants for your dining pleasure. Be sure to put South Pearl Street on itinerary.

DENVER TRAVEL GUIDE

Know Before You Go

Entry Requirements

The Visa Waiver Programme (VWP) allows nationals of selected countries to enter the United States for tourism or certain types of business without requiring a visa. This applies to citizens of the UK, Australia, New Zealand, Canada, Chile, Denmark, Belgium, Austria, Latvia, Estonia, Finland, Italy, Hungary, Iceland, France, Germany, Japan, Spain, Portugal, Norway, Sweden, Slovenia, Slovakia, Switzerland, Brunei, Taiwan, South Korea, Luxemburg, Singapore, Liechtenstein, Monaco, Malta, San Marino, Lithuania, Greece, the Netherlands and the Czech Republic. To qualify, you will also need to have a passport with integrated chip, also known as an e-Passport. The e-Passport symbol has to be clearly displayed on the cover of the passport. This secure method of identification will protect and verify the holder in case of identity theft and other breaches of privacy. There are exceptions. Visitors with a criminal record, serious communicable illness or those who were deported or refused entry on a past occasion will not qualify for the Visa Waiver Program and will need to apply for a visa. Holders of a UK passport who have dual citizenship of Iraq, Iran, Sudan, Syria, Somalia, Libya or Yemen (or those who have travelled to the above countries after 2011) will also need to apply for a visa. A requirement of the Visa Waiver Programme is online registration with the Electronic System for Travel Authorisation (ESTA) at least 72 hours before your travels. When entering the United States, you will be able to skip the custom declaration and proceed directly to an Automated Passport Control (APC) kiosk.

If travelling from a non-qualifying country, you will need a visitor's visa, also known as a non-immigrant visa when entering the United States for visiting friends or family, tourism or medical procedures. It is recommended that you schedule your visa interview at least 60 days before your date of travel. You will need to submit a passport that will be valid for at least 6 months after your intended travel, a birth certificate, a police certificate and color photographs that comply with US visa requirements. Proof of financial support for your stay in the United States is also required.

🌐 Health Insurance

Medical procedures are very expensive in the United States and there is no free or subsidized healthcare service. The best strategy would be to organize temporary health insurance for the duration of your stay. You will not need any special vaccinations if visiting the United States as tourists. For an immigration visa, the required immunizations are against hepatitis A and B, measles, mumps, rubella, influenza, polio, tetanus, varicella, meningococcal, pneumococcal, rotavirus, pertussis and influenza type B.

There are several companies that offer short-term health insurance packages for visitors to the United States. Coverage with Inbound USA can be purchased online through their website and offer health insurance for periods from 5 to 364 days. Visitor Secure will provide coverage for accidents and new health complications from 5 days to 2 years, but the cost and care of pre-existing medical conditions and dental care is excluded. Inbound Guest offers similar terms for periods of between 5 and 180 days and will email you a virtual membership card as soon as the contract is finalized. Physical cards will be available within one business day of arrival to the United States.

Traveling with Pets

The United States accepts EU pet passports as valid documentation for pets in transit, provided that your pet is up to date on vaccinations. In most instances, the airline you use will require a health certificate. While microchipping is not required,

DENVER TRAVEL GUIDE

it may be helpful in case your pet gets lost. If visiting from a non-English speaking country, be sure to have an English translation of your vet's certificate available for the US authorities to examine. To be cleared for travel, your pet must have a vet's certificate issued no less than 10 days before your date of travel. Pets need to be vaccinated against rabies at least 30 days prior to entry to the United States. If the animal was recently microchipped, the microchipping procedure should have taken place prior to vaccination. In the case of dogs, it is also important that your pet must test negative for screwworm no later than 5 days before your intended arrival in the United States.

In the case of exotic pets such as parrots, turtles and other reptiles, you will need check on the CITES (Convention on International Trade in Endangered Species of Wild Fauna and Flora) status of the breed, to ensure that you will in fact be allowed to enter the United States with your pet. There are restrictions on bringing birds from certain countries and a quarantine period of 30 days also applies for birds, such as parrots. It is recommended that birds should enter the United States at New York, Los Angeles or Miami, where quarantine facilities are available. The owner of the bird will carry the expense of the quarantine and advance reservations need to be made for this, to prevent the bird being refused entry altogether. Additionally, you will need to submit documentation in the

DENVER TRAVEL GUIDE

form of a USDA import permit as well as a health certificate issued by your veterinarian less than 30 days prior to the date of entry.

Airports

Your trip will probably be via one of the country's major gateway airports. **Hartsfield–Jackson Atlanta International Airport** (ATL), which is located less than 12km from the central business area of Atlanta in Georgia is the busiest airport in the United States and the world. It processes about 100 million passengers annually. Internationally, it offers connections to Paris, London, Frankfurt Amsterdam, Dubai, Tokyo, Mexico City and Johannesburg. Domestically, its busiest routes are to Florida, New York, Los Angeles, Dallas and Chicago. Delta Airlines maintains a huge presence at the airport, with the largest hub to be found anywhere in the world and a schedule of almost a thousand daily flights. Via a railway station, the airport provides easy access to the city.

Los Angeles International Airport (LAX) is the second busiest airport in the United States and the largest airport in the state of California. Located in the southwestern part of Los Angeles about 24km from the city center, it is easily accessibly by road and rail. Its nine passenger terminals are connected through a shuttle service. Los Angeles International Airport is a significant origin-and-destination airport for travellers to and from the United States. The second busiest airport in California is **San Francisco International Airport** (SFO) and, like Los Angeles it is an important gateway for trans-Pacific connections. It serves as an important maintenance hub for United and is home to an aviation museum. Anyone who is serious about green policies and environmentally friendly alternatives will love San Francisco's airport. There is a special bicycle route to the airport, designated bicycle parking zones and even a service that offers special freight units for travelling with your bicycle. Bicycles are also allowed on its Airtrain service. The third airport of note in California is **San Diego International Airport** (SAN).

Chicago O'Hare International Airport (ORD) is located about 27km northwest of Chicago's central business district, also known as the Chicago Loop. As a gateway to Chicago and the Great Lakes region, it is the US airport that sees the highest frequency of arrivals and departures. Terminal 5 is used for all international arrivals and most international departures, with the exception of Air Canada and some airline carriers under the Star Alliance or Oneworld brand. The Airport Transit System provides easy access for passengers between terminals and to the remote sections of the parking area.

DENVER TRAVEL GUIDE

Located roughly halfway between the cities of Dallas and Fort Worth, **Dallas-Fort Worth International Airport** (DFW) is the primary international airport serving the state of Texas. Both in terms of passenger numbers and air traffic statistics, it ranks among the ten busiest airports in the world. It is also home to the second largest hub in the world, that of American Airlines, which is headquartered in Texas. Through 8 Interstate highways and 3 major rail services, it provides access to the city centers of both Dallas and Fort Worth, as well as the rest of Texas. An automated people mover, known as the Skylink makes it effortless for passenger to transverse between different sections of the airport and the parking areas. Terminal D is its international terminal. The second busiest airport in Texas is the **George Bush Intercontinental Airport** (IAH) in Houston, which offers connections to destinations across the United States, as well as Mexico, Canada, the Americas and selected cities in Europe and Asia.

John F. Kennedy International Airport (JFK) is located in the neighborhood of Queens. In terms of international passengers, it is one of the busiest airports in the United States, with connections to 6 continents and with the air traffic of 70 different airlines. Its busiest routes are to London, Paris, Los Angeles and San Francisco. It serves as a gateway hub for both Delta and American Airlines. Terminal 8, its newest terminal, is larger than Central Park. It has the capacity of processing

DENVER TRAVEL GUIDE

around 1600 passengers per hour. An elevated railway service, the Airtrain provides access to all 8 of its terminals and also connects to the Long Island railroad as well as the New York City Subway in Queens. Within the airport, the service is free. Three other major airports also service the New York City area. **Newark Liberty International Airport** (EWR) is New York's second busiest airport and home of the world's third largest hub, that of United Airlines. Newark is located about 24km from Mid Manhattan, between Newark and Elizabeth. Its airtrain offers an easy way of commuting around the airport and connects via the Newark Liberty International Airport Station to the North Jersey Coast line and Northeast Corridor line. Other airports in New York are **La Guardia Airport** (LGA), located on the Flushing Bay Waterfront in Queens and **Teterboro Airport** (TEB), which is mainly used by private charter companies.

Washington D.C. is served by two airports, **Baltimore-Washington International Airport** (BWI) and **Washington Dulles International Airport** (IAD). Other important airports on the eastern side of the United States include **Logan International Airport** (BOS) in Boston, **Philadelphia International Airport** (PHL) and **Charlotte Douglas International Airport** (CLT) in North Carolina. The three busiest airports in the state of Florida are **Miami International Airport** (MIA), **Fort Lauderdale-Hollywood International**

DENVER TRAVEL GUIDE

Airport (FLL) and **Tampa International Airport** (TPA). In the western part of the United States, **McCarran International Airport** (LAS) in Las Vegas and **Phoenix Sky Harbor International** (PHX) in Arizona offer important connections. **Denver International Airport** (DEN) in Colorado is the primary entry point to Rocky Mountains, while **Seattle-Tacoma International Airport** (SEA) in Washington State and **Portland International Airport** (PDX) in Oregon provide access to the Pacific Northwest. **Honolulu International Airport** (HNL) is the primary point of entry to Hawaii.

Airlines

The largest air carriers in the United States are United Airlines, American Airlines and Delta Airlines. Each of these could lay claim to the title of largest airline using different criteria. In terms of passenger numbers, Delta Airlines is the largest airline carrier. It was founded from humble beginnings as a crop dusting outfit in the 1920s, but grew to an enormous operation through mergers with Northeast Airlines in the 1970s, Western Airlines in the 1980s and North-western Airlines in 2010. Delta also absorbed a portion of Pan Am's assets and business, following its bankruptcy in the early 1990s. Delta Airlines operates Delta Connections, a regional service covering North American destinations in Canada, Mexico and the United

DENVER TRAVEL GUIDE

States. In terms of destinations, United Airlines is the largest airline in the United States and the world. Its origins lie in an early airline created by Boeing in the 1920s, but the company grew from a series of acquisitions and mergers - most recently with Continental Airlines - to its current status as a leading airline. Regional services are operated under the brand United Express, in partnership with a range of feeder carriers including CapeAir, CommutAir, ExpressJet, GoJet Airlines, Mesa Airlines, Republic Airlines, Shuttle America, SkyWest Airlines and Trans State Airlines. American Airlines commands the largest fleet in the United States. It originated from the merger of over 80 tiny regional airlines in the 1930s and has subsequently merged with Trans Caribbean Airways, Air California, Reno Air, Trans World Airlines and, most recently, US Airways. Through the Oneworld Airline Alliance, American Airlines is partnered with British Airways, Finnair, Iberia and Japan Airlines. Regional connections are operated under the American Eagle brand name and include the services of Envoy Air, Piedmont Airlines, Air Wisconsin, SkyWest Airlines, Republic Airlines and PSA Airlines. American Airlines operates the American Airlines Shuttle, a service that connects the cities of New York, Boston and Washington DC with hourly flights on weekdays.

Based in Dallas, Texas, Southwest Airlines is the world's largest budget airline. It carries the highest number of domestic

DENVER TRAVEL GUIDE

passengers in the United States and operates over 200 daily flights on its 3 busiest routes, namely Chicago, Washington and Las Vegas. JetBlue Airways is a budget airline based in Long Island that operates mainly in the Americas and the Caribbean. It covers 97 destinations in the United States, Mexico, Costa Rica, Puerto Rico, Grenada, Peru, Colombia, Bermuda, Jamaica, the Bahamas, Barbados, the Dominican Republic and Trinidad and Tobago. Spirit Airlines is an ultra low cost carrier which offers flights to destinations in the United States, Latin America, Mexico and the Caribbean. It is based in Miramar, Florida.

Alaska Airlines was founded in the 1930s to offer connections in the Pacific Northwest, but began to expand from the 1990s to include destinations east of the Rocky Mountains as well as connections to the extreme eastern part of Russia. Alaska Airlines recently acquired the brand, Virgin America which represents the Virgin brand in the United States. Silver Airways is a regional service which offers connections to various destinations in Florida, Pennsylvania, Virginia and West Virginia and provides a service to several islands within the Bahamas. Frontier Airlines is a relatively new budget airline that is mainly focussed on connections around the Rocky Mountain states. Hawaiian Airlines is based in Honolulu and offers connections to the American mainland as well as to Asia. Island Air also serves Hawaii and enjoys a partnership with

DENVER TRAVEL GUIDE

United Airlines. Mokulele Airlines is a small airline based in Kona Island. It provides access to some of the smaller airports in the Hawaiian Islands. Sun Country Airlines is based in Minneapolis and covers destinations in the United States, Mexico, Costa Rica, Puerto Rica, Jamaica, St Maarten and the US Virgin Islands. Great Lakes Airline is a major participant in the Essential Air Service, a government programme set up to ensure that small and remote communities can be reached by air, following the deregulation of certified airlines. These regional connections include destinations in Arizona, Colorado, Kansas, Minnesota, Nebraska, New Mexico, South Dakota and Wyoming. In the past, Great Lakes Airline had covered a wide range of destinations as a partner under the United Express banner.

Hubs

Hartsfield Jackson Atlanta International Airport serves as the largest hub and headquarters of Delta Airlines. John F. Kennedy International Airport serves as a major hub for Delta's traffic to and from the European continent. Los Angeles International Airport serves as a hub for Delta Airline's connections to Mexico, Hawaii and Japan, but also serves the Florida-California route. Detroit Metropolitan Wayne County Airport is

DENVER TRAVEL GUIDE

Delta's second largest hubs and serves as a gateway for connections to Asia.

Washington Dulles International Airport serves as a hub for United Airlines as well as Silver Airways. United Airlines also use Denver International Airport, George Bush Intercontinental Airport in Houston, Los Angeles International Airport, San Francisco International Airport, Newark Liberty International Airport and O'Hare International Airport in Chicago as hubs.

Dallas/Fort Worth International Airport serves as the primary hub for American Airlines. Its second largest hub in the southeastern part of the US is Charlotte Douglas International Airport in North Carolina and its largest hub in the north is O'Hare International Airport in Chicago. Other hubs for American Airlines are Phoenix Sky Harbor International Airport - its largest hub in the west - Miami International Airport, Ronald Reagan Washington National Airport, Los Angeles International Airport, John F Kennedy International Airport in New York, which serves as a key hub for European air traffic and La Guardia Airport also in New York.

Seattle-Tacoma International Airport serves as a primary hub for Alaska Airlines. Other hubs for Alaska include Portland International Airport, Los Angeles International Airport and Ted Stevens - Anchorage International Airport. Virgin America

DENVER TRAVEL GUIDE

operates a primary hub at San Francisco International Airport, but also has a second hub at Los Angeles International Airport as well as a significant presence at Dallas Love Field. Denver International Airport is the primary hub for Frontier Airlines, which also has hubs at Chicago O'Hare International Airport and Orlando International Airport. Frontier also maintains a strong presence at Hartsfield-Jackson Atlanta International Airport, Cincinnati/North Kentucky International Airport, Cleveland Hopkins International Airport, McCarran International Airport in Las Vegas and Philadelphia International Airport. Honolulu International Airport and Kahului Airport serve as hubs for Hawaiian Airlines. Mokulele Airlines uses Kona International Airport and Kahului Airport as hubs. Minneapolis–Saint Paul International Airport serves as a hub for Delta Airlines, Great Lakes Airlines and Sun Country Airlines. Silver Airways uses Fort Lauderdale-Hollywood International Airport as a primary hub and also has hubs at Tampa International Airport, Orlando International Airport and Washington Dulles International Airport.

Seaports

The Port of Miami is often described as the cruise capital of the world, but it also serves as a cargo gateway to the United States. There are 8 passenger terminals and the Port Miami Tunnel, an

DENVER TRAVEL GUIDE

undersea tunnel connects the port to the Interstate 95 via the Dolphin Expressway. Miami is an important base for several of the world's most prominent cruise lines, including Norwegian Cruise Lines, Celebrity Cruises, Royal Caribbean International and Carnival Cruises. In total, over 40 cruise ships representing 18 different cruise brands are berthed at Miami. Well over 4 million passengers are processed here annually. There are two other important ports in the state of Florida. Port Everglades is the third busiest cruise terminal in Florida, as well as its busiest cargo terminal. It is home to *Allure of the Seas* and *Oasis of the Seas*, two of the world's largest cruise ships. Oceanfront condominium dwellers often bid ships farewell with a friendly cacophony of horns and bells. The third important cruise port in Florida is Port Canaveral, which has 5 cruise terminals.

With its location on the Mississippi river, New Orleans is an important cargo port, but it also has a modern cruise terminal with over 50 check-in counters. The Port of Seattle is operated by the same organization that runs the city's airport. It has two busy cruise terminals. The Port of Los Angeles has a state of the art World Cruise Center, with three berths for passenger liners. As the oldest port on the Gulf of Mexico, the Port of Galveston dates back to the days when Texas was still part of Mexico. Galveston serves both as a cargo port and cruise terminal.

DENVER TRAVEL GUIDE

🌐 Money Matters

🌐 Currency

The currency of the United States is US dollar (USD). Notes are issued in denominations of $1, $2, $5, $10, $20, $50 and $100. Coins are issued in denominations of $1 (known as a silver dollar, 50c (known as a half dollar), 25c (quarter), 10c (dime), 5c (nickel) and 1c (penny).

🌐 Banking/ATMs

ATM machines are widely distributed across the United States and are compatible with major networks such as Cirrus and Plus for international bank transactions. Most debit cards will display a Visa or MasterCard affiliation, which means that you may be able to use them as a credit card as well. A transaction fee will be charged for withdrawals, but customers of certain bank groups such as Deutsche Bank and Barclays, can be charged smaller transaction fees or none at all, when using the ATM machines of Bank of America. While banking hours will vary, depending on the location and banking group, you can generally expect most banks to be open between 8.30am and 5pm. You will be asked for ID in the form of a passport, when using your debit card for over-the-counter transactions.

While you cannot open a bank account in the United States without a social security number, you may want to consider obtaining a pre-paid debit card, where a fixed amount can be pre-loaded. This service is available from various credit card companies in the United States. The American Express card is called Serve and can be used with a mobile app. You can load more cash at outlets of Walmart, CVS Pharmacy, Dollar General, Family Dollar, Rite Aid and participating 7/Eleven stores.

Credit Cards

Credit cards are widely used in the United States and the the major cards - MasterCard, Visa, American Express and Diners Club – are commonly accepted. A credit card is essential in paying for hotel accommodation or car rental. As a visitor, you may want to check about the fees levied on your card for foreign exchange transactions. While Europe and the UK have already converted to chip-and-pin credit card, the transition is still in progress in the United States. Efforts are being made to make the credit cards of most US stores compliant with chip-and-pin technology. You may find that many stores still employ the older protocols at point-of-sales. Be sure to inform your bank or credit card vendor of your travel plans before leaving home.

🌐 Tourist Tax

In the United States, tourist tax varies from city to city, and can be charged not only on accommodation, but also restaurant bills, car rental and other services that cater mainly to tourists. In 22 states, some form of state wide tax is charged for accommodation and 38 states levy a tax on car rental. The city that levies the highest tax bill is Chicago. Apart from a flat fee of $2.75, you can expect to be charged 16 percent per day on hotel accommodation as well as nearly 25% for car rentals. New York charges an 18 percent hotel tax, as does Nashville, while Kansas City, Houston and Indianapolis levy around 17 percent per day hotel tax. Expect to pay 16.5 percent tax per day on your hotel bill in Cleveland and 15.6 percent per day in Seattle, with a 2 percent hike, if staying in the Seattle Tourism Improvement Area. Las Vegas charges 12 percent hotel tax. In Los Angeles, you will be charged a whopping 14 percent on your hotel room, but in Burbank, California, the rate is only 2 percent. Dallas, Texas only charges 2 percent on hotels with more than a hundred rooms. In Portland a city tax of 6 percent is added to a county tax of 5.5 percent. Do inquire about the hotel tax rate in the city where you intend to stay, when booking your accommodation.

🌐 Sales Tax

In the United States, the sales tax rate is set at state level, but in most states local counties can set an additional surtax. In some states, groceries and/or prescription drugs will be exempt from tax or charged at a lower rate. There are only five states that charge no state sales tax at all. They are Oregon, Delaware, New Hampshire, Alaska and Montana. Alaska allows a local tax rate not exceeding 7 percent and in Montana, local authorities are enabled to set a surtax rate, should they wish to do so. The state sales tax is generally set at between 4 percent (Alabama, Georgia, Louisiana, and Wyoming) and 7 percent (Indiana, Mississippi, New Jersey, Tennessee, Rhode Island) although there are exceptions outside that spectrum with Colorado at 2.8 percent and California at 7.5 percent. The local surcharge can be anything from 4.7 percent (Hawaii) to around 11 percent (Oklahoma and Louisiana). Can you claim back tax on your US purchases as a tourist? In the United States, sales tax is added retro-actively upon payment, which means that it will not be included in the marked price of the goods you buy. Because it is set at state, rather than federal level, it is usually not refundable.

Two states do offer sales tax refunds to tourists. In Texas you will be able to get tax back from over 6000 participating stores if the tax amount came to more than $12 and the goods were purchased within 30 days of your departure. To qualify, you need to submit the original sales receipts, your passport, flight or transport information and visa details. Refunds are made in cash, cheque or via PayPal. Louisiana was the first state to introduce tax refunds for tourists. To qualify there, you must submit all sales receipts, together with your passport and flight ticket at a Refund Center outlet.

Tipping

Tipping is very common in the United States. In sit-down restaurants, a tip of between 10 and 15 percent of the bill is customary. At many restaurants, the salaries of waiting staff will be well below minimum wage levels. With large groups of diners, the restaurant may charge a mandatory gratuity, which is automatically included in the bill. At the trendiest New York restaurants, a tip of 25 percent may be expected. While you can add a credit card tip, the best way to ensure the gratuity reaches your server is to tip separately in cash. Although tipping is less of an obligation at takeaway restaurants, such as McDonalds,

DENVER TRAVEL GUIDE

you can leave your change, or otherwise $1, if there is a tip jar on the counter. In the case of pizza delivery, a minimum of $3 is recommended and more is obviously appreciated. Although a delivery charge is often levied, this money usually goes to the pizzeria, rather than the driver. Tip a taxi driver 10 percent of the total fare. At your hotel, tip the porter between $1 and $2 per bag. Tip between 10 and 20 percent at hair salons, spas, beauty salons and barber shops. Tip tour guides between 10 and 20 percent for a short excursion. For a day trip, tip both the guide and the driver $5 to $10 per person, if a gratuity is not included in the cost of the tour. Tip the drivers of charter or sightseeing buses around $1 per person.

Connectivity

Mobile Phones

There are four major service providers for wireless connection in the United States. They are Verizon Wireless, T-Mobile US, AT&T Mobility and Sprint. Not all are compatible with European standards. While most countries in Europe, Asia, the Middle East and East Africa uses the GSM mobile network, only two US service providers, T-Mobile and AT&T Mobility aligns with this. Also bear in mind that GSM carriers in the United States operate using the 850 MHz/1900 MHz frequency

DENVER TRAVEL GUIDE

bands, whereas the UK, all of Europe, Asia, Australia and Africa use 900/1800MHz. You should check with your phone's tech specifications to find out whether it supports these standards. The other services, Verizon Wireless and Sprint use the CDMA network standard and, while Verizon's LTE frequencies are somewhat compatible with those of T-Mobile and AT&T, Sprint uses a different bandwidth for its LTE coverage.

To use your own phone, you can purchase a T-Mobile 3-in-1 starter kit for $20. If your device is unlocked, GMS-capable and supports either Band II (1900 MHz) or Band IV (1700/2100 MHz), you will be able to access the T-Mobile network. You can also purchase an AT&T sim card through the Go Phone Pay-as-you-go plan for as little as $0.99. Refill cards are available from $25 and are valid for 90 days. If you want to widen your network options, you may want to explore the market for a throwaway or disposable phone. At Walmart, you can buy non-contracted phones for as little as $9.99, as well as pre-paid sim cards and data top-up packages.

Canadians travellers will find the switch to US networks technically effortless, but should watch out for roaming costs. Several American networks do offer special international rates for calls to Canada or Mexico.

DENVER TRAVEL GUIDE

🌐 Dialing Code

The international dialing code for the United States is +1.

🌐 Emergency Numbers

General Emergency: 911 (this number can be used free of charge from any public phone in the United States).
MasterCard: 1-800-307-7309
Visa: 1-800-847-2911

🌐 General Information

🌐 Public Holidays

1 January: New Year's Day

3rd Monday in January: Martin Luther King Day

3rd Monday in February: President's Day

Last Monday in May: Memorial Day

4 July: Independence Day

1st Monday in September: Labour Day

2nd Monday in October: Columbus Day

11 November: Veteran's Day

4th Thursday in November: Thanksgiving Day

DENVER TRAVEL GUIDE

4th Friday in November: Day after Thanksgiving

25 December: Christmas Day (if Christmas Day falls on a Sunday, the Monday thereafter is a public holiday.) In some states, 26 December is a public holiday as well.

There are several festivals that are not public holidays per se, but are culturally observed in the United States. They include:

14 February: Valentine's Day

17 March: St Patrick's Day

March/April (variable): Easter or Passover

Second Sunday in May: Mother's Day

3rd Sunday in June: Father's Day

31 October: Halloween

Time Zones

The United States has 6 different time zones. **Eastern Standard Time** is observed in the states of Maine, New York, New Hampshire, Delaware, Vermont, Maryland, Rhode Island, Massachusetts, Connecticut, Pennsylvania, Ohio, North Carolina, South Carolina, Georgia, Virginia, West Virginia, Michigan, most of Florida and Indiana as well as the eastern parts of Kentucky and Tennessee. Eastern Standard Time is calculated as Greenwich Meantime/Coordinated Universal Time (UTC) -5. **Central Standard Time** is observed in Iowa, Illinois, Missouri, Arkansas, Louisiana, Oklahoma, Kansas,

DENVER TRAVEL GUIDE

Mississippi, Alabama, near all of Texas, the western half of Kentucky, the central and western part of Tennessee, sections of the north-western and south-western part of Indiana, most of North and South Dakota, the eastern and central part of Nebraska and the north-western strip of Florida, also known as the Florida Panhandle. Central Standard Time is calculated as Greenwich Meantime/Coordinated Universal Time (UTC) -6. **Mountain Standard Time** is observed in New Mexico, Colorado, Wyoming, Montana, Utah, Arizona, the southern and central section of Idaho, the western parts of Nebraska, South Dakota and North Dakota, a portion of eastern Oregon and the counties of El Paso and Hudspeth in Texas. Mountain Standard Time is calculated as Greenwich Meantime/Coordinated Universal Time (UTC) -7. **Pacific Standard Time** is used in California, Washington, Nevada, most of Oregon and the northern part of Idaho. Pacific Standard Time is calculated as Greenwich Meantime/Coordinated Universal Time (UTC) -8. **Alaska Standard Time** is used in Alaska and this can be calculated as Greenwich Meantime/Coordinated Universal Time (UTC) -9. Because of its distant location, Hawaii is in a time zone of its own. **Hawaii Standard Time** can be calculated as Greenwich Meantime/Coordinated Universal Time (UTC) -10.

DENVER TRAVEL GUIDE

🌐 Daylight Savings Time

Clocks are set forward one hour at 2.00am on the second Sunday of March and set back one hour at 2.00am on the first Sunday of November for Daylight Savings Time. The states of Hawaii and Arizona do not observe Daylight Savings Time. However, the Navajo Indian Reservation, which extends across three states (Arizona, Utah and New Mexico), does observe Daylight Savings Time throughout its lands, including that portion which falls within Arizona.

🌐 School Holidays

In the United States, the academic year begins in September, usually in the week just before or after Labour Day and ends in the early or middle part of June. There is a Winter Break that includes Christmas and New Year and a Spring Break in March or April that coincides with Easter. In some states, there is also a Winter Break in February. The summer break occurs in the 10 to 11 weeks between the ending of one academic year and the commencement of the next academic year. Holidays may vary according to state and certain weather conditions such as hurricanes or snowfall may also lead to temporary school closures in affected areas.

DENVER TRAVEL GUIDE

🌐 Trading Hours

Trading hours in the United States vary. Large superstores like Walmart trade round the clock at many of its outlets, or else between 7am and 10pm. Kmart is often open from 8am to 10pm, 7 days a week. Target generally opens at 8am and may close at 10 or 11pm, depending on the area. Many malls will open at 10am and close at 9pm. Expect restaurants to be open from about 11am to 10pm or 11pm, although the hours of eateries that serve alcohol and bars may be restricted by local legislation. Banking hours also vary, according to branch and area. Branches of the Bank of America will generally open at 9am, and closing time can be anywhere between 4pm and 6pm. Most post office outlets are open from 9am to 5pm on weekdays.

🌐 Driving

In the United States, motorists drive on the right hand side of the road. As public transport options are not always adequate, having access to a car is virtually essential, when visiting the United States. To drive, you will need a valid driver's licence from your own country, in addition to an international driving permit. If your driver's licence does not include a photograph,

DENVER TRAVEL GUIDE

you will be asked to submit your passport for identification as well.

For car rental, you will also need a credit card. Some companies do not rent out vehicles to drivers under the age of 25. Visitors with a UK license may need to obtain a check code for rental companies, should they wish to verify the details and validity of their driver's licence, via the DVLA view-your-licence service. This can also be generated online, but must be done at least 72 hours prior to renting the car. In most cases, though, the photo card type license will be enough. The largest rental companies - Alamo, Avis, Budget, Hertz, Dollar and Thrifty - are well represented in most major cities and usually have offices at international airports. Do check about the extent of cover included in your travel insurance package and credit card agreement. Some credit card companies may include Collision Damage Waiver (CDW), which will cover you against being held accountable for any damage to the rental car, but it is recommended that you also arrange for personal accident insurance, out-of-state insurance and supplementary liability insurance. You can sometimes cut costs on car rentals by reserving a car via the internet before leaving home.

The maximum speed limit in the United States varies according to state, but is usually between 100km per hour (65 m.p.h.) and 120km per hour (75 m.p.h.). For most of the Eastern states, as

DENVER TRAVEL GUIDE

well as California and Oregon on the west coast the maximum speed driven on interstate highways should be 110km per hour (70 m.p.h.). Urban speed legislation varies, but in business and residential areas, speeds are usually set between 32km (20 miles) and 48km (30 miles) per hour. In Colorado, nighttime speed limits apply in certain areas where migrating wildlife could be endangered and on narrow, winding mountain passes, a limit of 32km (20 miles) per hour sometimes applies. In most American states there is a ban on texting for all drivers and a ban on all cell phone use for novice drivers.

Drinking

It is illegal in all 50 states for persons under the age of 21 to purchase alcohol or to be intoxicated. In certain states, such as Texas, persons between the age of 18 and 21 may be allowed to drink beer or wine, if in the company of a parent or legal guardian. In most states, the trading hours for establishments selling alcohol is limited. There are a few exceptions to this. In Nevada, alcohol may be sold round the clock and with few restrictions other than age. In Louisiana, there are no restrictions on trading in alcohol at state level, although some counties set their own restrictions. By contrast, Arizona has some of the strictest laws in relation to alcohol sales, consumption and driving under the influence. The sale of alcohol is prohibited on Native American reservations, unless the tribal council of that reservation has passed a vote to lift restrictions.

🌐 Smoking

There is no smoking ban set at federal level in the United States. At state level, there are 40 states in total that enact some form of state wide restriction on smoking, although the exemptions of individual states may vary. In Arizona, California, Colorado, Connecticut, Delaware, Hawaii, Illinois, Iowa, Kansas, Maine, Maryland, Massachusetts, Michigan, Minnesota, Montana, Nebraska, North Dakota, New Jersey, New Mexico, New York, Ohio, Oregon, Rhode Island, South Dakota, Utah, Vermont, Washington and Wisconsin, smoking is prohibited in all public enclosed areas, including bars and restaurants. The states of Arkansas, Florida, Indiana, Louisiana, Pennsylvania and Tennessee do have a general state wide restriction on smoking in public places, but exempt adult venues where under 21s are not allowed. This includes bars, restaurants, betting shops and gaming parlours (Indiana) and casinos (Louisiana and Pennsylvania). Nevada also has a state wide ban on smoking that exempts casinos, bars, strip clubs and brothels. In Georgia, state wide smoking legislation exempts bars and restaurants that only serve patrons over the age of 18. Idaho has a state wide ban that includes restaurants, but exempts bars serving only alcohol. New Hampshire, North Carolina and Virginia have also introduced some form of state wide smoking restriction. While the states of Alabama, Alaska, Kentucky, Mississippi, Missouri, Oklahoma, South Carolina, Texas, West Virginia and Wyoming have no state legislation, there are more specific restrictions at city and county level. In Arizona, there is an exemption for businesses located on Native American reservation and, in particular, for Native American religious ceremonies that may include smoking rituals. In California, the first state to implement anti-smoking legislation, smoking is also prohibited in parks and on sidewalks.

Electricity

Electricity: 110 volts

Frequency: 60 Hz

Electricity sockets are compatible with American Type A and Type B plugs. The Type A plug features two flat prongs or blades, while the Type B plug has the same plus an additional 'earth' prong. Most newer models of camcorders and cameras are dual voltage, which means that you should be able to charge them without an adapter in the United States, as they have a built in converter for voltage. You may find that appliances from the UK or Europe which were designed to accommodate a higher voltage will not function as effectively in the United

States. While a current converter or transformer will be able to adjust the voltage, you may still experience some difficulty with the type of devices that are sensitive to variations in frequency as the United States uses 60 Hz, instead of the 50 Hz which is common in Europe and the UK. Appliances like hairdryers will usually be available in hotels and since electronic goods are fairly cheap in the United States, the easiest strategy may be to simply purchase a replacement. Bear in mind, that you may need an adaptor or transformer to operate it once you return home.

🌎 Food & Drink

Hamburgers, hot dogs and apple pie may be food items that come to mind when considering US culinary stereotypes, but Americans eat a wide variety of foods. They love steaks and ribs when dining out and pancakes or waffles for breakfast. As a society which embraces various immigrant communities, America excels at adopting and adapting traditional staples and adding its own touch to them. Several "Asian" favorites really originated in the United States. These include the California roll (offered in sushi restaurants) and the fortune cookie (chinese). Popular Hispanic imports include tacos, enchiladas and burritos. Another stereotype of American cuisine is large portion sizes. Hence the existence of American inventions such as the footlong sub, the footlong chilli cheese hot dog and the Krispy Creme burger, which combines a regular hamburger with a donut. Corn dogs are fairground favorites. Most menus are more balanced however. It is common to ask for a doggy bag (to take away remaining food) in a restaurant.

When in the South, enjoy corn bread, grits and southern fried chicken. Try spicy buffalo wings in New York, traditionally prepared baked beans in Boston and deep dish pizza in Chicago. French fries are favorites with kids of all ages, but Americans also love their potatoes as hash browns or the bite sized tater tots. Indulge your sweet tooth with Twinkies, pop tarts, cup cakes and banana splits. Popular sandwiches include the BLT (bacon, lettuce, tomato, the Reuben sandwich, the sloppy joe and the peanut butter and jelly.

Sodas (fizzy drinks) and bottled waters are the top beverages in the United States. The top selling soft drinks are Coca Cola, followed by Pepsi Cola, Diet Coke, Mountain Dew and Dr Pepper. In America's colonial past, tea was initially the hot beverage of choice and it was tea politics that kicked off the American Revolution, but gradually tea has been replaced by coffee in popularity. From the 1970s, Starbucks popularized coffee culture in the United States. Americans still drink gallons of tea and they are particularly fond of a refreshing glass of iced tea. Generally, Americans drink more beer than wine and favorite brands include Bud Light, followed by Coors Light, Budweiser and Miller Light. Popular cocktails are the Martini, the Manhattan, the Margarita, the Bloody Mary, the Long Island Ice tea and Sex on the Beach.

American Sports

Baseball is widely regarded as the national sport of America. The sport originated in the mid 1800s and superficially shares the basic objective of cricket, which is to score runs by hitting a ball pitched by the opposing team, but in baseball, the innings ends as soon as three players have been caught out. A point is scored when a runner has passed three bases and reached the 4th or home base of the baseball diamond. After 9 innings, the team with the highest number of runs is declared the winner. The Baseball World Series is played in the fall (autumn), usually in October, and consists of best-of-seven play-off between the two top teams representing the rival affiliations of the National League and American League.

Although the origins of American football can be found in rugby, the sport is now widely differentiated from its roots and today numerous distinctions exist between the two. In American football, a game is divided into four quarters, with each team fielding 11 players, although unlimited substitution is allowed.

DENVER TRAVEL GUIDE

Players wear helmets and heavy padding as any player can be tackled, regardless of ball possession. An annual highlight is the Super Bowl, the championship game of the National Football League. The event is televised live to over a 100 million viewers and features a high profile halftime performance by a top music act. Super bowl Sunday traditionally takes place on the first Sunday of February.

The roots of stock car racing can be found in America's prohibition era, when bootleggers needed powerful muscle cars (often with modifications for greater speed) to transport their illicit alcohol stocks. Informal racing evolved to a lively racing scene in Daytona, Florida. An official body, NASCAR, was founded in 1948 to regulate the sport, NASCAR. Today, NASCAR racing has millions of fans. One of its most prestigious events is the Sprint Cup, a championship which comprises of 36 races and kicks off each year with the Daytona 500.

Rodeo originated from the chores and day-to-day activities of Spanish cattle farmers and later, the American ranchers who occupied the former Spanish states such as Texas, California and Arizona. The advent of fencing eliminated the need for cattle drives, but former cowboys found that their skills still offered good entertainment, providing a basis for wild west shows such as those presented by Buffalo Bill. Soon, rodeo events became the highlight of frontier towns throughout the west. During the first half of the 20th centuries, organizations formed to regulate events. Today, rodeo is considered a legitimate national sport with millions of fans. If you want to experience the thrill of this extreme sport, attend one of its top events. The Prescott Frontier Days show in Arizona is billed to be America's oldest rodeo. The Reno Rodeo in Nevada is a 10 day event that takes place in mid-June and includes the option of closer participation as a volunteer. Rodeo Houston, a large 20 day event that takes place towards the end of winter, is coupled to a livestock show. Visit the San Antonio show in Texas during February for the sheer variety of events. The National Western Rodeo in Denver Colorado is an indoor event that attracts up to half a million spectators each year. The National Finals that takes place in Las Vegas during December is the prestigious championship that marks the end of the year's rodeo calendar.

Useful Websites

https://esta.cbp.dhs.gov/esta/ -- The US Electronic System for Travel Authorization
http://www.visittheusa.com/
http://roadtripusa.com/
http://www.roadtripamerica.com/

DENVER TRAVEL GUIDE

http://www.road-trip-usa.info/

http://www.autotoursusa.com/

http://www.onlyinyourstate.com/

http://www.theamericanroadtripcompany.co.uk/

Printed in Great Britain
by Amazon